AF435150

THE POWER OF DISCIPLINE

7 steps to reach your goals without relying on your motivation or willpower

Daniel J. Martin

ISBN 978-9916-9938-2-8

Disclaimer: This book has been created with the intention of providing information, suggestions, and guidance on various areas of life, including emotional well-being, mental health, personal growth, and the development of healthy relationships. However, it does not substitute for professional medical care or the advice of a qualified psychologist or therapist. If you are facing serious mental or emotional health issues, we recommend you seek professional help immediately.

"Discipline is the bridge between goals and accomplishment."

— Jim Rohn

CONTENTS

DOWNLOAD THE AUDIOBOOK FREE!

*If you would rather enjoy **The power of discipline** on the go, **you can download its audio version completely FREE!***

www.danieljmartin.es/audio/pod

INTRODUCTION

Why discipline?

Even though I don't know you, I know something about you: you can do so much more. How do I know that? Well, it's no secret: the vast majority of people are living beneath their potential. And if you're reading this book, I'm sure you're no exception.

I sense that there is something in your life that's not working. Maybe it's an important objective that's just out of reach, maybe you gave up on a dream and now you regret it, maybe you're disappointed by the life you lead or you feel that someone is taking advantage of you because you don't know how to take advantage of your resources and potential. Whatever it is, far from forgetting about it, I think it's weighing heavier on your mind every day.

Now, I want you to listen to me: you have the ability to achieve much more. Starting today. And I'm not talking about money or success (but those too!). I'm talking about true happiness. About being proud. About being amazed by achievements you never thought you could manage. This isn't all smoke and mirrors here, it's the actual truth: you can go so much further if you only discipline yourself.

Why discipline? What about passion, or willpower? Well, they're important too, just like intelligence and self-confidence, but if you truly want to be the master of your life, you need to learn to master your discipline.

So, what is discipline?

When we talk about discipline, we see a lot of skeptical eyebrows or even hackles raised. Discipline has so many negative connotations (submission, obedience, censorship, coercion, authoritarianism, punishment, loss of freedom...) that it's no wonder we tend to skip it and find alternative ways of getting what we want.

However, none of the above terms has anything to do with discipline understood as a tool for growth. The word "discipline" itself, derived from the Latin *discipulus* (disciple), has no relation to submission or punishment, but rather to learning: the root «disc-» corresponds to the Latin verb *discere* (to learn).

Discipline has to do with growing, not with obeying.

That is how businessman and educator Stephen Covey summed it up. The father-of-nine and author of the bestseller *The 7 Habits of Highly Effective People* said: "Most people equate discipline with an absence of freedom. In fact, the opposite is true."

Why? How can discipline be freedom if it forces us to do things we don't want to? How can someone who denies themselves sugar be freer than someone who stuffs their face with donuts whenever they want?

Discipline, when it is the fruit of a personal choice, is an attitude rather than an imposition. It is a mental tool that enables us to organize our everyday lives in order to progress toward our goals.

The more aspects of our daily lives we can control and discipline, the more efficient we will be and the better we will be at making the right decisions. Good decisions lead us to successes that boost our independence and freedom, and as such, discipline is not submission but rather a source of liberty.

Discipline shows you your true self

Formally, we could define discipline as a training method in any field, which guides us, gives us strength and prepares us to reach goals or optimal levels of knowledge in that field. So, discipline in your mission to learn a new language will consist of efficiently dedicating your time and attention to studying that language so that you can gradually master it. It's not a mystery.

However, in my years of experience advocating for discipline, I've seen its greater benefit: one that's much more elevated and powerful and which is not visible to most people at the beginning of the process. Discipline leads people to find their true selves in the most profound sense of the word.

This happens because discipline is an extraordinary road to knowing yourself. Discovering your strengths and weaknesses, your limitations and fears, what drives you in life and what you cast aside because it doesn't suit you: you will get to know all of this by practicing discipline. And I can tell you from professional experience that you're going to like your true self.

A disciplined person is highly aware of who they are and what their mission in this world is. An undisciplined person ends up living not just far beneath their potential, but far below who they truly are. A disciplined person is the captain of their ship; an undisciplined person is drifting with the current.

Discipline as a life raft

Discipline is also a powerful weapon for lifting us out of the pits that many of us unfortunately fall into at some point in our lives, through failure, loss of loved ones, past trauma, depression, and so on. Those of us who work in psychology know this well, and often prescribe high doses of discipline as a remedy for problems that threaten to sink people: when life beats you down, discipline can get you out of bed in the morning. Not because it gives you your hope back or because it heals your wounds, but because it's what you have to do in order to keep being you. Getting out of bed when there is nothing to fight for is a show of respect toward yourself.

I know that right now, you may be thinking that discipline can't change anything from your past or stop your boss from being so arrogant. But I'm sure you agree with this: being your own master empowers you to free yourself of the ghosts of your past and be more respected in the present.

Finally, always bear this in mind: if you don't discipline yourself so you can serve yourself, someone else will come along and discipline you so that you serve them instead. A person, a society, with an erratic and indulgent everyday life is easier to manipulate than someone who knows what they want and acts according to their own methods. If you feel that there is a part of you that is ruled by others (and I'm not talking about the reasonable obligations we all have in society, but about people taking advantage of your resources), discipline is your best weapon when it comes to setting boundaries.

Discipline is the opposite of leaving your time up to destiny. And destiny is a romantic enough concept for movies and books, but highly ill-advised in real life.

If everything I've said so far hasn't convinced you of how powerful discipline can be, I invite you to try it out for yourself: keep reading, and if following the 7 steps I suggest doesn't leave you more satisfied in your life, I'll give you your money back.

We all have objectives and dreams. We all want more fulfilled, productive and satisfactory lives. But we're not always sure what path we need to take. The aim of this book is to discover that path together. Because I believe I can help you – I once found myself in the same situation you might be in right now.

I invite you on a journey together toward a more fulfilling life. We will do this by choosing purposes and objectives that are worth having, and disciplining your actions so that they can lead you toward those objectives. We will look at how training your mind so that your impulses don't overcome you. And we will look at how to use your time, make the most of it and not get beaten down by life.

From the bottom of my heart, I hope you enjoy this exciting journey that may change your life.

Daniel

Examine your level of self-discipline

"I know nothing about surpassing others. I only know how to outdo myself."

— *Bushidō* Code (the book of Samurai warriors)

In September 2022, after twenty-seven years as a professional tennis player, Serena Williams announced she was retiring from the sport. She had won every tournament possible and become the best female tennis player of all time, as well as a shining example of empowerment for women and girls all over the world. Add to that the fact that she is a committed, family-oriented woman with integrity and solidarity, a multimillionaire who says she loves being a mother, and few people would fail to see her as the embodiment of success. How did she make it? Or rather, how did she make herself?

Without a doubt, her physical attributes helped a lot – but they were not the only factor. Her parents provided a lot of support in her childhood, but a devoted family is no guarantee of a child's success. Her intelligence? Yes, it was important, but not enough on its own. No, the factor without which Serena Williams could not have achieved the absolute record of twenty-three individual Grand Slam victories plus another seventy-three titles on top – the only indispensable factor in making her who she is – was her self-discipline.

Discipline **made the impossible possible.** Why do I say impossible? Because of the way things were when Williams first picked up a racket at three years old: what she would go on to achieve didn't even exist yet. No one had ever done it, especially not a black woman who had grown up in a city with one of the highest rates of crime and poverty in the country.

Serena Williams's self-discipline didn't just change her, it changed the world. It created space for someone who didn't exist yet. The impossible became possible.

Of course, when Williams started out, she wasn't planning on any of that. She probably had no idea what her mind and body were capable of, and I doubt that she was imagining the 260 million dollars she's worth today. Of everything that tennis was to bring her, the only part she knew was sweating through training, day after day.

The example of Williams helps me to demonstrate this: **discipline should be in our lives** ahead of willpower, vocation or faith. I'm not saying these elements aren't important – I'm saying they're no use if we don't align them with discipline.

Your turn!

It's time to talk about you. I'm guessing you're not Serena Williams, and that your accomplishments so far have been somewhat more modest. But in this chapter, we're not evaluating your past achievements – we're looking at the starting point for your future ones. In terms of self-discipline, do you know **your starting point right now**?

I invite you to take the following twelve-question quiz. Don't spend too much time on it; it's better if you don't think too hard about each answer:

1. Do you know your main **strengths** and **weaknesses**?

2. Do you **change your mind** easily?

3. Are your **thoughts**, **actions** and **wishes** for the future related to each other?

4. Do you spend more **money** than you should?

5. Do you know if you're **healthy**? (I'm not asking if you're healthy or not, I'm asking if you're aware of your current state of health).

6. Do you tend to break the **promises** you make to yourself or others?

7. Do you know your **fitness** level? (See question 5).

8. Do you believe you **deserve** better?

9. Do you know what your partner/friends/family **value** most about you?

10. When someone achieves something, do you feel that it's **unfair**?

11. Do you know what you **will be doing** next Tuesday at 5pm?

12. Do you find it hard to make **decisions**?

If you answered "yes" to most of the odd-numbered questions, it looks like your level of self-discipline is sufficient to get started. If most of your "yeses" were on the even-numbered questions...well, that's why you're reading this book!

Do you know yourself, or ignore yourself?

Now, I invite you to check on your relationship with yourself. Do you know yourself well? Do you ignore your own needs, or are you overindulgent with yourself? If you want, use this quiz as a guide:

1. Do you know your weaknesses?

What is stronger than you? What do you have no control over? Junk food? Your football team losing? Videogames? Your boss? Housework?

If you're not sure, observe yourself in your daily life. Work out when your weaknesses overcome you and in what circumstances or emotional states you turn to them. Write it down so you can keep it in mind.

2. Are you accounting for your limitations?

Limitations are the real obstacles you're starting out with, and they're a dose of either reality or humility: if you want to master surfing but you live two thousand miles away from the beach, you have an obvious limitation. If you want to play piano but you're missing two fingers, you'll have to focus your technique in another way. If you want to start a business but you can't afford the initial investment, you need to account for this limitation.

3. Where are your temptations?

Right now, I want you to look around your home, your phone, your place of work or neighborhood, and zoom in on the potential temptations around you. How far away from you are they? How easy is it for you to reach the weaknesses you noted down for the first question? What do you normally do to impede your access to them?

If you're constantly scrolling through apps that waste your time or money, delete them from your phone. If you go on websites that cause you problems, stop yourself from accessing them. Use a blocker, leave your phone in another room, turn it off: whatever you have to do.

If you walk past a bookmaker's or electronics store every day and it's causing issues for you, take another route.

4. Can you explain your goals and your plans for reaching them in one minute?

We still haven't talked about objectives, but I can tell you that once you have defined them, you will have to act accordingly. To do this, I suggest that you familiarize yourself with the elevator pitch technique.

The elevator pitch technique is used in the business sector to test whether an entrepreneur is clear on their project. It consists of "selling" the idea in the time it takes to take an elevator. If it doesn't manage to sound authentic or convincing, then either the person is unclear on their project, or they don't believe in it themselves.

Can you, in one minute, convince me that your objectives are achievable with your current lifestyle?

5. Do you have habits with feedback?

Sleeping well, eating healthy, working out, taking care over your appearance and keeping house are transversal habits that will help you with your goals, especially when willpower fails you or something you're leaning on falls for any reason: you can weather a storm better in a well-built, well-maintained house than in one that's falling to pieces. In good weather, both houses might look okay – but when the wind picks up, only the one that's ready for it will remain standing.

6. Do you treat yourself well?

Self-discipline doesn't mean self-harm. Life is also about those little pleasures after a long, hard day. Of course, these pleasures shouldn't interfere with your goals (if you're trying to lose weight, don't reward yourself with donuts), but you should treat yourself when you've worked hard.

If you're not in the habit of treating yourself, start now. You can list some little pleasures and, every morning, spend a few minutes enjoying them before your day begins. Anticipation is powerful and it will help to strengthen you.

Maybe everything I've said so far sounds like hyper life-coach talk. A handful of healthy habits isn't going to turn you into a different person, and going back to the example of Serena Williams, you're not three years old and you can't demand huge changes of your brain at this point in your life.

We tend to believe that once we reach adulthood and have formed our characters, **we can't change** no matter how disciplined we are. If you think that too, let science show you you're wrong.

What does neurology say about discipline?

In recent decades, the relationship between discipline and brain function has been studied in great depth, with groundbreaking results.

As you know, your brain is formed of various regions with different functions. At the front of your skull, behind your forehead, is your prefrontal cortex. This is the most modern zone from an evolutionary point of view and is responsible for **executive functions**. These are the things we do consciously and voluntarily after a complex cognitive process: making decisions, organizing daily tasks, adapting our social behavior to each situation, and so on.

Executive functions guide our behaviors and enable our attention, planning and adaptation of actions as we go, thanks to information we obtained on previous occasions (what we call "working memory") and in accordance with the goals we set ourselves.

How does self-discipline affect all those executive functions? **Self-discipline trains your mind** to carry them out more efficiently when the time comes. It's a toolkit you have at your disposal.

Research using brain imaging shows a clear correlation between levels of **self-discipline** and **brain activity**: when you perform any executive function, the more self-discipline you have, the better the activity in your prefrontal cortex, which means your brain is handling more options for tackling the task.

Let's look at an example. In the face of temptation (like your phone vibrating with a new message while you're driving), your brain quickly starts working to provide a response. A disciplined prefrontal cortex will have more information on past situations and will conclude that it's not worth taking your attention off the road to look at the message: consequently, you as a driver will ignore that temptation without much effort. In a person with less self-discipline, the way they act has no guideline, so their brain won't know whether to respond to the temptation or not: consequently, the driver will hesitate and probably pick up their phone while driving, because it's easier to give in to temptation than to resist it.

Self-discipline helps you **stay focused**. Even in the face of unknown stimuli, a disciplined brain has more clues on how to act than one forced to constantly improvise. In other words: a disciplined brain has a better hand of cards to play.

Self-discipline and identity

Self-discipline doesn't just guide you when it comes to everyday tasks – it helps you to **be who you are**.

We are not born with self-discipline; it's a skill we learn and memorize when we are young, until it becomes a part of us. If you were to suddenly erase that learning from your mind, your character would change and you would stop being you.

You have probably heard of the famous case of the US railway worker Phineas Gage, who on September 13 1848 suffered a serious accident at work that destroyed part of his frontal lobe. Apparently, while he made a full recovery – he could walk, eat, talk, and so on – those close to him said "**he was never the same again**". Phineas, a pleasant and formal man, became an impulsive, rude, and chaotic blasphemer.

This shows that all his training on how to behave had been erased from his hard drive. Given that being responsible and formal defined Phineas, when he stopped being responsible and formal, he stopped being Phineas.

Following this logic, if discipline is part of what we're like, can discipline **turn us into someone we're not yet** but who we would like to be?

The answer is most definitely yes.

This was demonstrated by a study into neuroplasticity: the brain *always* has the capacity to improve its neural organization. In fact, it is known that the brain is capable of continuing to generate neurons and neural connections **until we are more than eighty years old**.

Until recently, in the same way that you "got" the pair of legs that you got (slim, long, strong, and so on), you also "got" a frontal lobe with the limits and capacities that you got. This was unless you had a terrible accident like Phineas did, a neurodegenerative disease, or something else with a similar impact which meant you couldn't change your executive efficiency no matter how hard you tried, much less improve it.

However, we now know that executive functions can be trained and improved on a voluntary basis at any life stage. That means that our **intelligence** and **personality** are not set in stone: we have power over them.

It's true that your personal and genetic history mold your frontal lobe in one way or another, but neither your DNA nor your past have the last word: **you do**.

Self-discipline starter kit

Before moving on to the next chapter, I would like to know if you already have a self-discipline starter kit in your daily life. I'm talking about the **set of habits** you should already have: something like what you typically get with a car.

So, what are these habits? There is no official list, so let me tell you the ten that I consider essential:

1. Get up **early** in the morning and always at the same time, whether or not you have somewhere to be.
2. Spend between **six and eight hours a day** on your main productive activity, whether that's work, study or raising your children while they're little.
3. **Exercise** regularly.
4. Get enough **sleep**.
5. Eat a **balanced** diet.
6. Practice **self-care**, both at a health level and in terms of personal appearance and caring for your home.
7. Cultivate and maintain healthy social **relationships**, both within and outside of your family.
8. Be a **responsible** and respectful citizen toward your community and those around you.
9. Have **free time** and enjoy it.
10. Have goals.

This baseline will help you much more than you think: these habits **feedback on themselves** and prepare your brain to welcome other habits that are more difficult to sustain over time and for which you will require more **perseverance**.

Chapter summary

- **Discipline should be in your life** with more presence than willpower, passion or faith.

- Discipline is a tool that will help you to perform your executive functions **more efficiently**.

- To discipline yourself, you must know yourself: what are your **strengths** and **weaknesses**, your **limitations, goals, plans, habits** and **relationship** with yourself.

- Treat yourself **fairly**: self-discipline is synonymous with growth, not punishment.

- Studies into **neuroplasticity** have shown that we can change voluntarily at any stage of life through self-discipline.

Find your life purposes

"The two most important days in your life are the day you are born and the day you find out why."

— Mark Twain

"But why, some say, the Moon? ... We choose to go to the Moon in this decade and do the other things, not because they are easy, but because they are hard; because that goal will serve to organize and measure the best of our energies and skills."

This was the forceful speech of John F. Kennedy on September 12 1962 at Rice University, Houston, when he literally promised Americans and beyond the moon.

This chapter is dedicated to your life purpose, or your own personal Moon. If you're still not sure what that is, now is the time to find out.

What are life purposes?

Life purposes (also known as meanings or profound motivations) are the **ultimate** things we live for. They are the personal, voluntary missions that give existence itself a sense of identity and direction; they help us to know who we are and what our place is in the world. Life purposes relate to the main decisions we make in life and they cannot be imposed on us by others.

When I talk about life purposes, I tend to cite the neurologist and psychiatrist Viktor Frankl, who survived a Nazi concentration camp. In his book *Man's Search for Meaning*, considered one of the most influential books in the US, he suggested something that he had discovered in the camps: prisoners who maintained their will to live despite the calamities facing them were those who had a **reason why**. The author himself, who lost his entire family in the camps, stated that he would not have survived if not for his determination to write his book.

In the words of Nietzsche, "he who has a why to live for can bear almost any how."

What's your reason why?

If you truly want to change something in your life, if you want to achieve new things, you need to know what your motivation is for doing so. Being a good parent, writing a novel, keeping the family business going, passing a test, overcoming anxiety...Everything you set your mind to requires sacrifice. **The greater the**

sacrifice, the more powerful your reason why will have to be.

Your reason why doesn't necessarily need to be epic or capable of changing the course of history. It just needs to be important enough to you that it'll keep you fighting for it.

Life purpose versus happiness

I often hear that our life purpose is to be happy. Without a doubt, happiness is one of the most logical things to fight for, but it's **risky** to equate it with the meaning of life, because there are so many variables we can't control. In reality, happiness is simply an **added benefit** that we obtain from living focused on our purpose.

The real reasons why we choose to lead one life or another should not be related to achieving a happy life, but rather to **who we want to be**.

What would you do if you had no fear?

I tend to ask my patients this question when they are unsure of their purposes or life meanings. Their first responses are usually timid and extraordinarily cautious. I have to keep insisting, encouraging them to say "silly" things until they admit the **wishes they had silenced** through years of trying to be "realistic". The answers they give then make their eyes shiny and their smiles wide: "to open a creative bakery", "to be a business coach", "to design boats", "to start a new life on another continent", "to have a big family", and the like.

We all have something **we're good at** or which **we deeply yearn for**. Something we like doing, or that we can do for hours without getting tired. When we can, we make that our life's direction. If we're less lucky, we do something with it in our free time.

Do you know what you're good at, or what you yearn for most? Is it close to being a purpose in your life? Bear in mind that doing something you love is reason enough to do it, no matter the outcome.

Here are some examples of the **purposes** of people I know who are proud of their lives:

- To be a good neurologist.

- To be the best teacher I can be.

- To form a family where every member is loved and respected.

- To improve life for people in my town.

- To fight climate change.

- To create a revolutionary videogame.

- To start a band.

- To organize a sporting event that makes it big and keeps going for years.

- To keep my ancestors' traditional lifestyle going so it doesn't get forgotten.

- To open a play center for deaf-mute children.

Your purposes in reverse

If you're still unsure of your life purposes, I suggest to you a reverse exercise: don't think about what you want to achieve, but **what you want to *avoid***. It could be something like:

- I want to avoid financial hardship.
- I want to avoid having a boring job.
- I want to avoid any profession that's not related to X.
- I want to avoid a life that has no positive impact on society.
- I want to avoid ending up like X person.

If you are sincere, you'll see that the path you need to follow will become clearer.

Watch out for your lizard brain!

All the research into the topic agrees on this: people who have a life purpose are happier, have better self-esteem and enjoy better relationships with those around them. However, there are people who interpret that purpose as **esoteric** or "just for people with an easy life", because they perceive it as a **threat** to their already delicate life balance.

To an extent, this is justified. And it tends to happen in these circumstances:

- Physical or emotional **exhaustion**.
- Physical **pain** or **sickness** that worries or limits you.
- **Stress, post-traumatic stress** or **burnout**.
- Ongoing **financial** difficulty.
- **Lack of information** on how to achieve that purpose.
- **Fear of success** or imposter syndrome.

- **Incompatibility** between the purpose and the requirements of your current environment.

In situations like these, identifying with purposes that go beyond getting to the weekend is so hard to do, because our primitive brain – the one that takes care of keeping us alive and which is still intact after 250 million years of evolution – prioritizes our immediate wellbeing over some hypothetical future benefit. Our **survival instinct** is, then, in opposition to our **life purpose**.

In fact, you don't even need to be in an extreme situation in order to activate your lizard brain: catch the flu, and you'll strongly protest against anything other than lying in bed.

If you're going through a hard time, be aware of that. Treat yourself with **compassion** if you're self-flagellating because of low productivity or a lack of dreams to fight for. It'll come. Realize that your lizard brain is **protecting** you, and reach an agreement with it.

In the next chapter, we'll look at another step that comes before self-discipline: **commitment** to your purpose or mission. Give your word that you will commit, and there will be no turning back: this is how you want to be in the future, and it will be so.

Chapter summary

- Life purposes are the **ultimate reasons** we live for.

- Happiness should not be a life purpose in itself, but rather a positive **side effect** of living with purpose.

- Living without purpose is living **beneath your potential**.

- In difficult times, your primitive brain **prioritizes survival** ahead of future benefits.

Commit to your mission

"The most important element in the failure equation is your personal commitment to keep trying."

— Catherine Pulsifer

Got your life purpose(s)? Congratulations! That's a very important step on your growth journey. Now, it's time to commit to it, knowing there will be stumbling blocks along the way.

In an ideal world, there would only be correct decisions, because we would weigh up all the variables in advance so we couldn't make mistakes. But sadly, we're in the real world, and we can never be **certain** that we're taking not just the right path, but also the right mission for us. How could we possibly know for sure?

Nothing is 100% certain, which is why we psychologists encourage people to act once they are **75% sure** that it's the right thing to do. That 75% is enough to justify a commitment: that prevents the need to be totally sure (which is impossible) from becoming an eternal **excuse** to do nothing.

Another way to be aware of what your mission truly involves is to frame it as if you were signing a contract with the bank: in other words, read the **fine print** with a magnifying glass.

The fine print of your purpose

We all remember the property crisis that began in 2008 and swallowed up the savings of thousands of families. There were many factors involved, but one was especially painful: banks were persuading people on low incomes to buy houses they couldn't afford. It was a scam, but legal.

Why? Because the fine print in the contract that everyone **signed without reading** explained what they weren't telling people: that those buyers would be up to their eyeballs in debt and that the banks would repossess their houses at the first sign of trouble.

If people had been aware of what those contracts involved, they never would have signed. But they got swept up in the banks' serious image, because it was what everyone was doing, because they kept hearing people say that houses never went down in value, because of their wishful thinking – because we're all human, basically. And people (including relatives of mine), did something you should never do: they **committed blindly**.

This is why I insist on the importance of knowing what your commitment to your chosen purpose will involve. If you want to be an actor, some of the main clauses of your contract will be about feeling validated, getting famous, winning awards, playing unique characters, and traveling. But the fine print will tell you about the hours spent memorizing boring scripts, voice training exercises, early mornings, initial uncertainty, harsh critics and the fact that absolutely nothing is guaranteed. These are the things you need to weigh up before committing to an acting career – not the number of premieres you'll get invited to.

If you're not sure what the fine print of your purpose is, I recommend you find out using questions such as:

- Do you know the **action** you will most have to perform? (For example, if you want to be a boxer, that action is probably bouncing on the balls of your feet.)

- Do you know what you will have to **give up** before, during and after you achieve your purpose?
- Do you know the proportion of **luck** or unpredictable events involved in your mission?
- Do you have **mentors** or people around you with a similar mission?
- What would mean **failure** at your mission? What would mean **success**?
- What is the **worst** that can happen?
- Where do you **draw the line** with your mission? In other words, in what situation would it be braver to give up than to keep going?

Knowing what you're facing will reduce your chances of quitting when you encounter hurdles along the way.

Bury your excuses

"If you really want to do something, you'll find a way. If you don't, you'll find an excuse."

— Jim Rohn

To commit to your objective, it's essential that you stop **kidding yourself**. More than keeping to a strict timetable, more than dedicating X number of hours to your work, commitment requires honesty with yourself. And if there's one thing that means you're not being honest, it's excuses.

We all invent excuses to **get out** of doing something we don't want to do, or to **forgive ourselves** for something we did wrong. It's inevitable in a society that constantly demands that we give our time to others. But the number of excuses we use regularly says a lot about us: it tells us whether we are **trustworthy** or not, and if we lead lives that are more or less organized and **aligned** with our goals.

When someone says: "I couldn't come to your event because my car broke down", they're saying that the breakdown caused their inevitable absence at the event and that, had it not been for the car, they would have been there. Is that an excuse, or a valid reason?

It depends on that person's intentions. If the car really was their only way of getting there and it really did break down, then it was a **cause outside their control**. If the car didn't break down, or it broke down and that person **took advantage** of the situation to get out of the event rather than seeking alternative transport, then it's an excuse.

Here's a list of the main excuses my patients use to avoid taking action. If you're living in "excuse mode" too, I recommend that you acknowledge it.

- **The past:** It's true that many people are dealt a bad hand in life. Injustice, trauma and misfortune place some people far behind others in the starting line toward success. If that's you, remember that **taking action will help you**. You might not be able to fight on every front you'd like to, but don't stop showing up for battle: you'll see that life comes round. Remember that you're not your past, nor does your past determine your future.

- **The way of the world:** Unlike the above excuse, this one doesn't tend to be used by those who were dealt a bad hand, but rather those who have a better and **bigger comfort zone**. Complaining about the government, about how people behave, about the times, about violence in the world, and so on is valid, but doing nothing because "it's not worth it" is not.

Simply by refining your sense of observation, you'll realize that those who most complain about and lament the state of the world are those who contribute the least to improving it. If you're one of these people, evaluate the extent to which you're part of the **problem** and not the **solution**.

- **I'm not ready:** This is laudable when it's legit. If you don't feel ready for a relationship, a more ambitious job or a marathon, it's better to say so. However, if you really want something, set yourself a **deadline** and detail the **necessary requirements** to be ready by then. If you don't, you're just getting bogged down in excuses.

- **It won't work:** People who use this excuse specialize in **sabotaging their own dreams** and those of others. Under the pretext of "you've gotta be realistic", they kill amazing projects before even taking the first step. Yes, you have to keep your feet on the ground, but living in paralysis because you know something won't work is silly. Remember that, unfortunately, we are not **fortune tellers**.

"It won't work" hides a terrible **self-fulfilling prophesy.** A self-fulfilling prophesy is a defensive mechanism that's more or less conscious and which we deploy in order to cause something to fail, just like we "predicted" it would. The problem is that that prediction is not based on objective facts, but on distorted or outright false intentions and interpretations.

- **I'm really bad at it:** Statements along the lines of "I'm so bad at…" or "I'm no use at…" sometimes reflect distorted beliefs about our own capabilities, but usually they're just excuses not to try something. To stop these thoughts, I usually quote Jim Rohn: "Don't say 'If I could, I would.' Say 'If I can, I will'."

- **I already tried:** It's true that failure is demoralizing. If you already tried and failed, it's better to leave it, right? Well, no: it's wise to pick your battles, but not picking any at all is underestimating yourself.

Before you give up, you need to take that failure that hurt so much down to the autopsy table and figure out what went wrong. Then, assess the relationship between that failure and what you're trying to do today. If the objective is the same (for example, running a marathon), you need to **learn from experience** and tackle it more efficiently the next time. Remember the quote from the beginning of this chapter: you're committed to keep trying.

- **It's too late for that:** Yes, time takes its toll. We're no longer those whippersnappers brimming with energy and passion who could rule the world. Our ships have sailed; we need to accept that. Are you someone who thinks this way? Then remember what we said about neuroplasticity: **it's never too late to be who you want to be**.

When I tell my patients this, they often react with sarcasm: "What, so I could still be the next Mozart?". I ask them if they really want to be the next Mozart, and the answer is always no; we don't want to be other people, we want to be ourselves, just with better performance.

In terms of your limitations, all I can say is this: it is proven that even an alcoholic's frontal lobe has the ability to recover completely and **go back to full capacity** once the addiction has been beaten.

What's really behind a lot of excuses is **fear**. It's risky to take a leap, but you have to try. Don't always believe it's "better the devil you know" – in fact, don't ever believe it.

What is motivation and why should it play the best side role?

It's said that the toughest training ever was that of samurai men and women. Not only were they physically prepared from childhood, but they were also subjected to testing of their ability to endure pain, cold, hunger and exhaustion and taught elevated mental control over their impulses and emotions. If those warriors, who tended to be from wealthier classes (hence not needing to go through hardship in order to live), could bear all of that, it was because they identified with and *believed in* what they were doing.

How can you identify with your life purpose? What do you need to do to ***believe in it***?

You need **motivation**.

Let's go back to Kennedy's lunar program and an anecdote that took place in 1963, when JFK visited NASA to check up on their progress. It's said that, while touring the facilities, Kennedy bumped into a member of the cleaning team and asked him about his work duties. The janitor replied, "Mr President, I'm helping put a man on the Moon."

The anecdote demonstrates not just the commitment of that worker to the company, but above all, it shows what motivation is: with his duties so distantly related to aerospace engineering, the janitor felt that he was a part of the Moon landing project and was therefore totally committed to his job (essentially, mopping the floors).

Over the past fifty years, there have been many studies into motivation. In the work arena, they all tend to throw up similar to results than those suggested by the NASA janitor: money is a great incentive but, once a worker has a suitable salary guaranteed and enjoys job security, it's the type of duty, focus and result that provide (or don't provide) motivation. Out of two janitors on the same salary with the same responsibilities, we will find that the one working at a place he finds interesting is much more motivated. The other janitor may well be content and satisfied, but the first is *motivated*. Which of them will be better at resisting temptation when it comes knocking?

If motivation is such a powerful force, why self-discipline? Isn't it enough to be motivated?

Excellent question. It's true that, without motivation, it's very hard to accept any self-discipline at all. The problem is that motivation depends on a lot of emotional and social factors, so it's unstable. Self-discipline, on the other hand, occurs regardless of emotions, so it's much more mechanical and less liable to change.

In other words: if self-discipline is the vehicle driving us toward our dreams, motivation is the spark that gets the engine running.

Focus on identity

The concept of identity has been closely studied by James Clear in his work on the creation of habits. For Clear, as for many other writers (myself included), success comes when you **identify with your mission**, in other words you *become* the person who manages to accomplish that mission. If you want to be a musician, adopt the mindset of someone who is already become a professional musician. Forget about the objective you'll reach in a few years and focus on a change of identity: bring the future into the here and now.

This may all sound a little abstract. In his book *Atomic Habits*, Clear explains it with the following example: two smokers have decided to quit. When someone offers them a cigarette, they both decline, although their answers are subtly different: the first says "no thanks, I'm trying to quit", and the other says "no thanks, I don't smoke". We all know that talk is cheap, but **attitude** is not: the first smoker is battling his addiction but has not changed his mindset (he still doesn't see himself as a non-smoker), while the second already identifies as the **new him** that he wants to be.

The effect of well-founded progress, or not starting from scratch

This technique is based on the fact that people commit more easily to a task **if they have already completed some of it**.

It's been proven in numerous experiments, often in schools with poor academic performance.

At such schools, students tend to have very bad relationships with their studies, because studying brings them no joy and because they don't identify with the purpose of studying.

Here, the technique consists of telling students at the beginning of the year that they all already passed with the highest grade: a ten out of ten, an A+, whatever the maximum is in that educational system. Of course, the students think it's a trick and are unmoved: they know it's not possible. In any case, they have never achieved an A in anything. But it's guaranteed to them, and they talk about how they feel about having that A-grade.

Then they are told that all they have to do throughout the year is defend that A-grade. Tests, classwork, quizzes, any assessment of their learning: these are the dangers they need to watch out for. Every time they fail, they have to give up a little bit of that A and watch their grade drop a little.

The idea of offering them an A-grade off the bat is to incentivize them to view themselves as students with good grades. The chance at ending the year with a pass, a C or even an A rather than yet another fail grade makes committing to their mission seem **much more appealing**.

Keep your mortality in mind

This morbid phrase leads me to mention another of the teachings of the samurais' Bushidō code: to progress toward success, you must always bear the idea of death in mind. Since we're not samurais, we don't need to think about physical death, but rather a **potential casualty**. Why?

Many psychological studies have shown that the strongest commitment to a mission happens when you imagine the **worst-case scenario**. Visualizing the negative as a possibility, far from discouraging or alarming you, provides you with an extra dose of maturity.

If your wish in life is to be an independent business owner, try visualizing a disappointing future: for example, working jobs far beneath your potential (this doesn't mean that is what is going to happen). If you still decide to pursue it, that visualization will help you in times of **frustration**.

Committing to the future means leaving the past behind

Another drama: cutting off your past. Leaving your old life behind forever to commit to a life goal is not only difficult on an emotional level, but also a rational one. It's not about leaving your small town for the big city but *keeping* the same mentality – it's about adopting a **new mentality**, which means leaving the old one behind forever.

All living things feel an instinctive drive to behave according to our **actions from the past that brought us benefits**, or at least that allowed us to avoid pain. When we make a decision that involves ending these actions, our brains reject it, because it's part of the brain's job to keep us safe above all else. That's why it won't hesitate to protest and invent excuses, sophisticated or otherwise. One such excuse is the famous imposter syndrome.

Imposter syndrome

Imposter syndrome is a fear of success. It involves a **false belief** linked to low self-esteem, whereby we do not believe in our own worth or we do not think we deserve others' trust in the objective we have set ourselves, whether in the professional arena or in romantic or family relationships.

Our brains get ahead by making us feel unworthy of what we have achieved or are about to achieve as a defense mechanism against a greater evil: the pain and shame of being "found out" or rejected by our colleagues or relatives because we tried to do something we didn't *deserve*.

To escape this syndrome, you have to work on your self-esteem and prove to yourself in ways no matter how small that you *are* worth it and that you are worthy of trust.

Hand-in-hand with imposter syndrome is the fear of being **abandoned by our group** if our growth awakens jealousy or envy. Sadly, that is inevitably going to happen and you will have to hear those dreaded words: "you've changed".

Commit to yourself no matter who it annoys. I'm not talking about being selfish or opportunistic or about stepping on people's toes: I'm talking about the fact **your mission should be respected** in the same way that you should respect others' missions, too.

Don't waste time trying to convince people that, even though you're undergoing personal or professional growth, you're still worthy of their love or trust. Those who care about you will stay by your side, and those who don't were only around to use you anyway.

Don't move on to the next chapter if you still haven't committed to an objective. It doesn't need to be your big life purpose right now: you can simply commit to **personal improvement.** You will see that on the path to self-discipline, you'll find your reason why.

Chapter summary

- Before committing to your goal, you need to read the **fine print** of that commitment.

- Excuses delay you in **taking action**. You should understand their short-term benefit and long-term danger.

- **Motivation** is what pushes you to take that **first step**. Self-discipline is what enables you to **keep going**. That's why you need the former to *believe* and the latter to *arrive*.

- Motivation belongs to the realm of **desire**, whereas self-discipline belongs to the realm of the **rational**.

- Identifying with your **future self** enables you to commit more naturally.

- Keeping the **unpredictable** in mind (your mortality) is important in maturing your life projects.

- Committing to change means **cutting off your past**.

- Fear of the unknown gives rise to **imposter syndrome** and other false beliefs.

Discipline your body

"We must all suffer from one of two pains: the pain of discipline or the pain of regret."

— Jim Rohn

In the next two chapters, we will focus on techniques and resources for introducing self-discipline to your body and mind. Remember that your mind encompasses two facets: intellectual activity, and emotional activity.

The good news is that all three – body, rational thinking and emotion – are interconnected and feed into each other, so by improving one, you will also benefit the others.

In this chapter, you will learn to conquer your body's resistance to physical effort in order to become healthier, happier and more efficient.

Our bodies instinctively flee from pain and take shelter in pleasure. However, we know that the "pain" of getting in shape is not harmful, but rather the opposite – while the "pleasure" of a sedentary lifestyle is going to catch up with you in the long term.

Imagine you're getting ready to run a race. One of your objectives is to make your body endure a little more each day. How do you convince it to do this? How, when you've run the ten miles that you managed yesterday, do you tell it that it can run a little further?

The 40% rule SEALs use

You already know the SEALs: members of the US Navy's elite unit. In a sense, SEALs are the modern-day equivalent of samurais: the best-prepared fighters in the country.

During the tough training to become a SEAL, candidates use the **40% rule**: when they feel they have reached the limits of their physical strength, they assume that in actual fact **they have only used 40% of it**. In other words, they still have another 60% to go before their bodies reach true exhaustion, though that 60% will be painful, their lizard brains ringing every alarm bell.

If you do not know yourself well enough, you don't know where your **physical limit** is, so you allow yourself to be guided by the alarms your brain rings at the first sign of tiredness. As a consequence, way before your body gets exhausted, you buy into the **belief** that you can go no further.

Interestingly, that belief can be easily **manipulated** by your mind. Placebo experiments have demonstrated that athletes given a "caffeine" pill (that actually contains no active ingredients) at the point at which they hit the wall are capable of continuing, believing that it is due to the extra boost of energy from the pill – in actual fact, it is nothing but self-suggestion.

This proves that **their bodies could keep going**, even when their brains said they could not.

You can apply the 40% rule to your workouts in addition to many other situations in your everyday life: that last meeting of the day when you're already exhausted, the football practice you promised your son, the walk home carrying heavy grocery bags... Simply put, whenever you believe you can't keep going, remember that you still have **half your energy reserves left**[1].

---

[1] This doesn't mean you should risk your safety or integrity, or that you can disobey medical orders. The 40% rule should be applied to healthy habits as a self-discipline technique.

Master your pain

The way we perceive physical pain is different for everyone, depending on our personalities, genes, emotions and prior experiences. However, it is possible to **modify your pain threshold** using mental techniques in order to make it more bearable.

Instinctively, our first impulse when faced with pain is to try to get away from it however we can: moving the affected area around (what do you do when you shut your finger in a door?), exhaling, yelling, cursing... Many of these actions are not aimed at stopping the pain, but rather at **distracting your mind** so that it perceives the pain less intensely. And it works.

Distracting the mind is the basis for most pain relief strategies[2]:

---

[2] It's important to note that the only pain I don't recommend you ignore is that of voluntary exertion, which doesn't apply to injuries, accidents or sickness.

- **Observe your pain:** This consists of focusing on painful sensations and feeling how they come and go even when you do nothing to stop them. There will come a point at which you feel able to bear the pain without reacting, and it will become less intense.

- **Imagine your body** as a channel or path down which the pain moves like a cable or water pipe.

- **Breathe** deeply and consciously for as long as the pain lasts, just like you do when meditating.

- Visualize **calming images** or a very near future event (for example, your weekend workout).

- **Downplay the pain** by comparing it to pain you've felt before or pain you imagine to be worse. You may find the words of triathlete Javier Gómez Noya helpful here: "The only part of my body that hasn't hurt me during training is my eyelashes."

One of the most intense types of pain experienced in our society is that which women experience **during childbirth**. The contractions, which last hours, intensify during the final stages, which is precisely when women are exhausted and yet must find the strength to push.

I mention this because it's linked to my **favorite technique** for mastering pain: all I have to do is remember that my mom, who had far less preparation than me, was able to endure such intense pain while giving birth to me, so I can endure the physical pain of any discipline I inflict on myself.

Discipline your nights

One of the worst things we're doing as a species is keeping **terrible sleeping habits**.

Sleep is one of our most basic needs, and the list of ailments caused by not getting enough of it is endless. Nevertheless, my patient list is full of people who don't know how to get enough rest, and not many of them take the problem seriously enough.

Why don't we sleep as much as we should?

Most people cite the same reasons: stress, anxiety, physical pain, worries, imbalance between mental and physical tiredness, too much stimulation, light, noise, and so on. I know these reasons well; they are the same ones I used before I disciplined myself on sleep.

However, I doubt that we have **worse sleeping conditions** than people did in the Middle Ages. Back then, people were colder, sicker and perpetually hungry or going to bed facing numerous threats: wolves or rats, to name but a few relatively common situations. I say this to reflect on whether what's stopping you sleeping today is truly impossible to change.

I tend to ask my patients if they knew that SEALs can fall asleep in two minutes, even if they're sitting up in broad daylight with bombs exploding around them. Obviously, they tend not to have known that and I say it just to get a reaction; I don't actually want anyone to have to fall asleep amid gunfire.

What I really want to do is **minimize** my patients' reasons. Not because their anxiety or pain is not important, but because **it's not important at bedtime**.

Any thought or emotion that crosses your mind once you've decided it's time to sleep is working against you, and you need to know how to make it go away.

The pad on your nightstand

Some patients tell me that it's when they're in bed that they remember important things they need to do the next day or are suddenly struck by great ideas. Others tell me that anxiety sets in just as they're trying to sleep. This happens because our nervous systems are so **destabilized** by stress that they avoid sleep just in case there's "something else to do". Our **guard is up** all the time.

A good way of telling your brain it can relax now is to keep a pad on your nightstand and note down any thoughts that come to you in just a couple of words, cutting off any further thoughts on the matter. What you're telling your hypervigilance is: "OK, noted, you can go to sleep, we'll look at that tomorrow."

Apply this technique and it won't be long before your brain stops mulling things over right before you sleep, because it knows you've noted them down for the next day and that you won't forget about them.

The SEALs' sleep technique

As I mentioned, elite American soldiers are trained to fall asleep pretty much any time and in any situation. To do this, they use relaxation techniques that enable them to quickly lower their **melatonin** levels.

Melatonin is a hormone we generate naturally and which affects our sleep cycles. Levels increase at dusk, when the light fades, and decrease during the initial hours of sleep. Peak melatonin occurs between **8pm and 10pm** (this varies depending on the season and geographical location).

The function of melatonin is to facilitate **sleep latency**, which is the time it takes you to fall asleep (the dreaded **falling asleep** stage).

Sleep latency of **up to twenty minutes** is considered normal in children and young people, and **up to thirty minutes** in adults and older people.

What SEALs do is reduce the duration of this phase as much as possible by relaxing their body zone by zone, as if unplugging appliances.

This is an adaptation of their relaxation guidelines, although you can find many others online and on audio platforms. Of course, like many techniques, this doesn't work straight away; it takes some practice.

1. Lie down on the bed, close your eyes and visualize the various areas of your face without moving them. Relax them one by one: forehead, eyelids, under-eye area, nose, lips...

2. Do the same for your shoulders, arms, neck, hands and fingers in turn. If you feel that these areas are tense, forcibly tense them for a few moments and then relax them.

3. Be aware of your lungs for a few seconds.

4. Relax the lower half of your body, visualizing it without moving: your abdomen, pelvic region, legs, feet.

5. Focus on your mind and picture something very relaxing, like rocking gently in a canoe on calm waters. If this doesn't work, picture the phrase DON'T THINK and repeat it to yourself for a few minutes.

Other tricks to disciplining your resting habits

- Keep to the same routine every day.

- Make your bedroom a nice place: calm, quiet, tidy, with the right temperature and no electronic devices plugged in at night.

- Give your latency phase time: if you want to sleep seven and a half hours, don't go to bed right when you have seven and a half hours before your alarm goes off.

- End the day with a guided sleep relaxation exercise.

- End the day with an exercise in gratitude or congratulate yourself for the effort you made during the day. I recommend trying the *gratitude journal* I use with my patients:

Chapter summary

- You must learn to discipline your body and mind, which involves physical, intellectual and emotional activity.

- The **40% rule** is based on the belief that you can't physically go any further, when in actual fact you have over half your **energy left**.

- You can reduce your **perception of pain** using mental techniques.

- Good **sleep habits** are basic and have repercussions on all your physical, mental and emotional functions.

Discipline your mind

"Rule your mind, or it will rule you."

— Horace

Now, let's take a look at how we can get your head in order by training your **intellectual resources and emotional side**. Bear in mind that the connections between the two – your thoughts and your emotions – are so strong that it is impossible to discipline one without also educating the other.

Let's begin with the rational side of things.

Your intellectual resources

Any intellectual activity, from writing a report to reading the instructions for an electronic device, requires **concentration**. However, we spend our days subjected to endless mental stimuli and our brains are working tirelessly to interpret and curate the information they receive – this tends to cause **stress** and **distraction**.

Stress causes hormones such as cortisol to be released. These hormones, when released in excess, lead to memory problems and changes in mood and can cloud our mental clarity when it comes to making decisions.

Can you make friends with your stress?

Surprisingly, the answer is yes. Not only *can* you make friends with your stress: you must!

Stress is simply an adaptive response to a situation. In the case of a test, **feeling a little stressed** (or under pressure) is a good thing, because it helps keep you **focused** on the test. However, if you are so afraid of failure that your stress levels go through the roof, this excessive stress can cause **mental block**. So, your first battle in the fight to discipline your mind is not against stress itself, but against **excessive stress**.

It's an important distinction.

Stress is not about having too much work to do – it's about feeling like you can't manage it. The sensation of suffocation is the difference between effective people and those who, with the same amount of time available to them (a day has twenty-four hours no matter who you are), suffer and fail.

Remember the example of the two houses in the storm from chapter one? Well, when you live your life perpetually under a storm, you can't just patch up the brickwork – you have to work on the foundations. And, if necessary, you have to demolish the entire house and rebuild it on firmer foundations. This sometimes means deconstructing beliefs you had been clinging to.

The fight against neural discomfort

Neural discomfort is a sensation similar to the pain from the 40% rule, but which appears **before we begin a task**: it tends to crop up when we're faced with tedious, boring, unpleasant, or long jobs, even if they are not physically exhausting.

Experiments show that if we **ignore these messages** and simply get straight to work, neural discomfort disappears within a few minutes or even seconds and we can perform the task with efficiency and concentration.

How can you combat **neural discomfort**?

The first thing to do is to be aware of it. Remember that when your brain is trying to protect you from danger (even when that danger doesn't really exist), it won't hesitate to **lie to you**. That's good news, because it means your self-protection system is working. The bad news is that you need to be able to tell when your brain is tricking you.

The second thing to do in order to beat neural discomfort is to learn to endure the first minute of the task **even though you are uncomfortable with it**. You will experience tiredness and negative emotions in that time, and side with your brain: in essence, you just don't like doing it (but you keep going).

Every time you continue to undertake a task in spite of your neural discomfort, your brain realizes that there was no danger after all, so it will be easier each time. When you have repeated that action or habit a hundred times – whether that's training for a marathon, showering in cold water or negotiating hard on a financial deal, your brain will stop sending you messages telling you to stop, because it's learning that **there is no real danger**. What you're telling your brain is: "don't worry, it's under control."

Try to practice some **uncomfortable activities** every day. Not as self-flagellation, but to familiarize yourself with that unpleasant sensation. If you want to get in shape, take the stairs. If you want to improve your social skills, force yourself to have brief conversations with people outside your circle every day. If you want to get really good at cooking, force yourself to use foods you don't love or which are not very versatile.

The Pomodoro Technique

This famous resource helps to keep you from feeling worn out at the thought of spending the next few hours or days performing a horrible, boring or mentally exhausting task. It was invented by the Italian Francesco Cirillo, and its name (which means "tomato") came about because the technique involved using a kitchen **timer** that looked like a tomato.

The technique consists of introducing a few minutes of controlled pleasure into maximum concentration time with a view to oxygenating your brain. Cirillo suggested **five minutes of rest for every twenty-five of concentration**, but you can adapt this to suit your needs.

During those breaks, you can do anything except concentrate. You can dance, practice deep breathing, go out onto your balcony, laugh with a friend, have a snack or a drink... (Don't start tasks you have to leave half-done if that makes you nervous.)

Cirillo also suggested taking a longer break every four "pomodoros".

Before you begin, you need to calculate the number of hours you are going to spend on the task and decide how regular your breaks will be, then set your timer for them. It's important not to change either the work intervals of the breaks throughout the exercise: if you decide on a 30-5-30-5 schedule, stick to it. If you can go past twenty-five minutes to thirty-five or forty-five without your performance dropping, do it. Self-discipline **feeds on repetition**.

Lobdell's waves of concentration

The psychologist Marty Lobdell, an expert in study techniques, suggested something very similar to the above method. To study for five hours at maximum concentration (in other words, when you understand and retain as much information as possible), he claimed we needed six hours. For every half hour of study, you get five minutes of free time.

Why interrupt that rhythm? Won't that distract you?

Experiments have shown that after thirty minutes of maximum concentration, it begins to **drop**. A graph of the trajectory of concentration would show a curved line gradually descending after the first half-hour which does not go back up. Your risk of being distracted by things around you or by intrusive thoughts shoots up, which is why Marty Lobdell suggests taking a break to get some air.

After five minutes, your brain is ready for another half-hour.

If you follow Lobdell's technique, the concentration line would rise and fall in the shape of five waves: one for each study/pause unit. It is true that the last half-hour will never be as productive as the first, but it will be better than if you forced yourself to maintain your concentration for five hours straight.

Self-discipline for your emotions

It's time to look at the hardest part of self-discipline according to most of my patients (you'll soon realize it's not actually the hardest, but it is the scariest).

I've already explained that self-discipline acts in accordance with a **decision made previously**, not feelings that come up during the action.

But can you affect emotions themselves? Can you *not feel* something?

Actually, no. But you *can* **educate** your behavior or reaction, and you've been doing that since you were a kid.

Many people try to overcome their emotions by ignoring them. I believe the key is to do the opposite: just as you need to know your physical limitations, you should **know your emotions and their triggers**.

For example, if you experience road rage, you need to know in advanced that emotions such as rage and anger will rear their ugly heads if you end up stuck in rush-hour traffic. The solution is not to avoid this, but to **face it**: get in that jam one day when you're not in a hurry, and wait for those emotions to come. Feel the desire to yell, to pummel the steering wheel or even to get out of your car, looking for a fight. Acknowledge that these are your emotions, but they're not *you*.

Another technique I recommend in situations that drive you crazy is what I call:

"commentating on the game". It consists of **describing** what you're going through (for example, the traffic) as if you were commentating on a football game from the stands.

It might sound silly, but if you repeat this technique regularly, you'll find your road rage stops coming back and you'll save yourself some precious energy.

Annoy yourself

This relates to the famous emotional comfort zone. It's about leaving aside the feelings and emotions that make you feel safe, and seeking out those that annoy and bug you. Once again, you're not trying to turn your life into an ordeal, but rather to **accept unpleasant emotions** as part of the furniture so that they don't throw you off your balance when they crop up unexpectedly.

Here are some ideas that my patients have used to help them get used to irritating emotions:

- If you can't abide **embarrassment**: Dance in the middle of the street or wear a bright color all day.

- If you find **public speaking** hard: Talk to people on the bus or subway and ask them if they've seen an umbrella you just lost.

- If you need to **be in control** in order not to be nervous: Spend one whole day handing over control and the initiative to others.

- If you hate things that **aren't to your taste**: Listen to a song you can't stand, walk a little way with a stone in your shoe, talk to someone about a topic on which you know their opinion is the polar opposite of yours, go eat at a restaurant that you think is overpriced.

The gray rock technique

Some situations – actually, people – simply get to us. These tend to be **toxic or manipulative** people who enjoy playing mind games and watching others blow up. If you have someone like this in your life and it's not possible for you to cut them out – which would be my preferred option – I recommend that you learn the gray rock technique.

The mantra of this technique is ***respond, don't react***. It's about not giving people the attention or argument they're looking for, because your intentions are different from theirs: you might be arguing in order to clear the air, but they're just secretly enjoying watching you fly off the handle.

Instead of getting sucked into an argument, **turn down the volume on your emotions** to zero and become an unmovable gray rock: use neutral phrases with no personal implications, be ambiguous when provoked and answer with lukewarm expressions (it's possible, uh-huh, maybe, I guess, I'm not sure) and so on. If the other person becomes more aggressive, don't change your stance: I'm sorry to hear you say that, I don't see it that way, I can't change your mind, what do you mean by that?, and so on.

At first, you'll feel insincere, and I'm sure the other person will notice it too. But with practice, you can learn to become the gray rock that troublemakers and difficult people trip up on.

Discipline against anxiety

Put succinctly, your anxiety is your lizard brain sending **warning alarms**. The problem is that your alarm system has been hacked, and now it's sending you signals even when there is no real risk to your survival.

I could write at least one entire book on the topic of anxiety, but for now I'm just going to dedicate a section to some basic recommendations for tackling it.

1. Talk to it

Talk to your anxiety when you feel it. Treat it as if it were an inconvenient visitor you need to get rid of quickly but politely: "I'm sorry, now's not a good time", "I understand why you're here, but I don't need you right now."

2. Use relaxation techniques

There are many resources, from meditation to writing therapy. If you undertake a relaxing activity when your anxiety is at its peak, it will pass more quickly: remember, anxiety is fleeting and it disappears once it has delivered its "message".

3. Show it that you can

Anxiety is your own insecurity telling you you can't. Don't get mad about it; remember, it's just your brain trying to protect you. Find ways to win **small victories** in order to gain in confidence and show your anxiety that you can. If your problem is with public speaking, start by talking to a couple of your neighbors about something. Then, increase your audience to three or four people in a range of situations. If you're terrified of swimming in the ocean, get a summer calendar and commit to submerging a little more of yourself in the water each day.

4. Confront your anxiety with a diagnosis

Anxiety sometimes comes in the form of chest pains or episodes of "crazy". To unmask it, go to the doctor and get tests to prove that all you're experiencing is an anxiety attack, not a heart attack or sickness.

Chapter summary

- Disciplining your mind means training both the **intellectual part** and the **emotional part**.

- **Stress** and **excessive stress** are not the same thing: stress (tension) helps keep you focused. Excessive stress blocks and overwhelms you.

- **Neural discomfort** is that uneasy feeling you get before beginning a task you don't feel like doing.

- **Study techniques** such as the Pomodoro are basic in maintaining concentration at any intellectual activity.

- To discipline your emotions, you need to **acknowledge** them without judgement and anticipate their **triggers**.

- You can't stop yourself from **feeling something**, but you can dominate your emotions so they don't stand in your way.

- Anxiety is just the **messenger**.

Mold your time

"Time is a created thing. To say 'I don't have time,' is like saying, 'I don't want to."

— Lao Tzu

Everything we own and everything around us is **made of time**. The dinner you're going to eat tonight, your professional career, the Great Pyramids of Egypt: they are all made of the time they took to be created.

However, the amount of time used to do things has not always been the most efficient: in fact, I believe the human race is the species that **wastes** the most time throughout our lives.

Why can't we make the most of time?

Parkinson's Law

Have you ever felt that the bigger your home is, the more you fill it with stuff? Well, the same thing happens with time: if you have a lot of time to complete a task, you will probably fill that time with side jobs and still only make your deadline by the skin of your teeth.

This is what British historian Cyril Parkinson discovered in 1957 in terms of administrative tasks: we tend to increase the amount of work in a task until **we have filled the time** given to us to complete it. And, on the flipside, if the time available to us is reduced, we are capable of effectively simplifying a task in order to get it done on time.

It is because of this principle that people tend to say they work better under pressure, or that without a deadline looming, they can't seem to get to work. In reality, you should not accept this. If you can do something in an hour, you shouldn't make it take all afternoon, even if you have that afternoon available. Self-discipline also means deciding in advance how much time you will spend on a task (remember, time doesn't come out of a vending machine – it comes out of your life) and sticking to it.

> "The bad news is time flies. The good news is you're the pilot."
> — Michael Altshuler

I don't have time!

A teacher once decided to show his students that time is much more organic than we tend to believe. He got a jar and began to put rocks inside it. When the jar was full, he asked:

"Do you think anything else will fit in here?"

His students shook their heads.

So the teacher got a fistful of gravel and dropped it inside the jar. The smaller stones ran between the rocks, filling the empty space until no more could fit. Once again, the teacher asked:

"Now, can any more fit in?"

His students shook their heads.

The teacher got hold of some fine sand and began to pour it into the jar. The gaps that the gravel hadn't been able to fill were soon packed with sand. When the sand reached the top of the jar, he asked again.

"What about now? Can I put anything else in?"

His students shook their heads again.

Finally, the teacher poured water into the jar, managing to get a good glug in before it overflowed.

The jar is your time, and what you put inside the jar are the things you spend our time on. The rocks are the most important things (yourself, your family, your career, and so on) and they are what should receive the most time. But between them, there is space for much more if you know how to adapt it to the jar: the gravel, sand and water are all the other things that fill your life, from friends and leisure to travel, distant cousins, housework or puppy training.

I invite you to think about what your rocks, gravel, sand and water are. Then, calculate the amount of time you spend on each of them. Do you like what you see?

If you analyze your daily time distribution, from when you get up in the morning to when you go to bed, and if you're like most mortals, I think you'll notice two things:

1. Significant **drains** on your time, especially surrounding cellphone use, videogames or shopping, during the week, and uninteresting activities on the weekend.

2. **Empty space** you're not making the most of and which you could spend doing things you like (the spaces still in the jar after you add the gravel and the sand): your daily

commute, time wasted standing in line or in waiting rooms, and the like.

There's nothing wrong with using social media, going shopping, meeting up with friends or lying on the couch doing nothing. The problem is doing those things when you had planned to do something else, or doing them for longer than you should when you know you're going to regret it.

The 10 commandments of time management

1. **Thou shalt use your agenda every day:** every night, you will plan the next day, and every morning you will check your list before your day begins.

2. Thou shalt consider your **long-term agenda**, the one with life goals in it.

3. **Thou shalt plan** every week, month and year when it begins.

4. Thou shalt ask yourself often: what is the most **important** thing I need to do right now?

5. Thou shalt fight in equal amounts against **perfectionism** and **procrastination**.

6. Thou shalt learn to **place boundaries** on the demands of others and on social pressures.

7. Thou shalt not **give your time** to people who do not deserve it.

8. Thou shalt keep things that **waste your time** under control.

9. Thou shalt learn to do what you can already do, **faster**.

10. Thou shalt **resist** Parkinson's Law.

Productive time management

"I find it fascinating that most people plan their vacations with better care than they plan their lives. Perhaps that is because escape is easier than change."

— Jim Rohn

Below are the recommendations I usually make when it comes to maximizing your time at work or in business:

- Define and write the **three most important tasks** of the day. Begin the day by working on them, starting with the one that requires most concentration.

- **Assign** a time limit to each task. Set **reasonable deadlines**.

- **Concentrate 100% on each activity**: whether you're checking a spreadsheet or chatting with a friend, during that time, nothing else matters.

- Reduce **interruptions**: don't check your email every two minutes. Instead, decide how often you're going to look at your inbox.

- Do in one block all the little tasks that you can **finish in less than three minutes** (to get rid of the distraction they cause).

- If you have an unpleasant task pending, get it out of the way **early on** in the day.

- **Classify** and order the rest of your tasks. I recommend Stephen Covey's method:

  1) Urgent and important.

  2) Important but not urgent.

  3) Urgent but not important.

  4) Neither urgent nor important.

- **Leave space** in your agenda for delays or unforeseen events.

- Learn to **delegate**, **trust** in others' abilities and **ask for help** when necessary.

- Learn to **say no** to unreasonable requests. We all do favors and we all like to help, but no one deserves to be used.

- Remember to take **breaks** and not become **hyper-focused** (it's one thing to concentrate and quite another to miss your lunch break or leave work late because you're so engrossed in your task).

- Keep your work space clear.

- At the end of each day, **evaluate** the day as if it you were assessing a football team after the game.

- If you hate your job, remind yourself often **why you work**. Don't feel like the world owes you anything for your efforts: 98% of the population makes about as much effort every day as you do.

The Pareto principle

The **Pareto** principle states that 80% of consequences come from 20% of causes, 80% of results come from 20% of the work and 80% of a company's profits are generated by 20% of their products and clients.

If we apply this law to time management, we see that 80% of the results that interest you **come from just 20% of your productive time**. Pinpoint that time and eliminate the tasks that don't benefit you.

For example, if you work out ten hours a week, but you spend some of that time choosing what to wear, taking selfies for social media, recording yourself explaining your workout session and talking to friends at the gym, don't say that you spend ten hours actually getting fit.

Let it be known that I'm not judging the way you work out. What I want to know is: is that the way you want to do it?

If you can discipline your mind and emotions, you should be able to discipline your time so that it serves you and not the other way around.

Chapter summary

- We tend to use **all the time available to us** for a task, whether we need it or not (Parkinson's Law).

- In order to be more productive, it's essential that you **plan** each day, month and year in advance.

- According to the **Pareto principle**, just 20% of the time you spend working provides 80% of the desired results.

- At work, **delegating**, **prioritizing** and **ignoring** what's not important at that moment will save a huge amount of time.

- Ask yourself regularly: what is **important** that I do right now?

Conquer temptation

"The temptation to give up is greatest right before you are about to succeed."

— Chinese proverb

Ancient Greek mythology tells us that sirens were evil beings who lived out at sea and had beautiful voices. They enjoyed tempting sailors, drawing them out to sea where they would trap and drown them.

It also tells the story of Ulysses, who knew of the danger and ordered his crew to plug their ears with wax so that they couldn't hear the sirens' song when they passed by. However, he didn't want to miss out on hearing their beautiful voices, so he asked to be tied to the mast and left there no matter how much he demanded to be untied.

In the end, when they passed by Siren Island, Ulysses heard the voices tempting him with sweet promises, but the sirens were unable to drag him away, since he was tied up.

I mention this legend because you can't always keep the siren song away. The best way to face temptation is to know that it exists and to use strategies to resist it, rather than naïvely believing you can simply look the other way.

The next section is about precisely this.

Siren islands

Just as Ulysses knew he would have to sail past Siren Island, you know that certain situations will tempt you. The best thing to do is avoid them, but as we've said, that's not always possible; that's why you need a **backup plan** for when you know you have to sail past the sirens.

Backup plans are actions you mentally draw up in advance in order to tackle a situation you know is going to be difficult. Psychologists call this technique **"implementation intention"**, and it works a little like a prompt at a theater, whispering actors' lines to them when they go blank on stage.

Let's say you're on a diet and Christmas is coming up. You know that an important part of social gatherings at this time is eating and drinking in excess. A possible backup plan is **deciding in advance** that you will only have one plate of food and one drink at each celebration. Picture yourself doing this and keeping busy chatting to relatives or colleagues in order to avoid eating any more.

Having a backup plan will help you to control the adverse situation and save energy on having to **improvise** or **rely on your emotional state** to resist temptation: remember that temptations come when you let your guard down, and they do it seemingly innocently: "it doesn't matter if you cheat on your diet for one day. You only live once!".

Remember: sailors who listened to the siren song drowned.

The ten-million-dollar check

This technique is taken from an anecdote attributed to actor Jim Carrey.

It's said that for many years, Carrey would carry a ten-million-dollar check in his wallet. That check was written on a napkin, so its true value was exactly zero dollars.

Carrey dreamed up this supportive strategy when he was just starting out, working unpleasant, badly-paid jobs and facing an uncertain future. He put the "check" in his wallet and, every time he got his wallet out, he would see the check and remember **the future he wanted.** That kept at bay his temptation to abandon his acting career and get a "real" job. Well, it's now estimated that Jim Carrey is worth 150 million dollars.

I invite you to design your own check (there are templates for this) with the value you think you should receive for devoting your life to your mission. Carry it with you and look at it any time you're tempted to give up.

Other tricks to avoiding temptation

By now you will have realized that your brain is going to try to keep you away from the arduous journey of self-discipline by any means possible. That's why it's important that you reinforce your decisions with every trick you can learn for resisting temptation. Here are a few more:

1. **Give your word.** Find somebody you would hate to disappoint and tell them what you're trying to achieve. Committing your honor and pride will help you to keep going.

2. **Put your money where your mouth is.** Decide on an amount of money it would really hurt you to lose, and give it away every time you fail. For example: every time you don't complete a task, you will transfer a hundred dollars to your team's rivals or the political party you detest the most.

3. **Mark every successful day on a calendar** and hang it somewhere visible. Little by little, the calendar will fill up with small wins, and it'll hurt more and more when you let yourself down.

4. **Surround yourself with the right people**. Behavior is contagious. Our decisions are influenced by the people around us much more than you think: surround yourself with people who help you and whom you can help, and you'll feel the difference.

5. **Big Brother.** Use your cellphone to record yourself from the moment you've decided to complete an annoying task (like cleaning out the refrigerator or answering emails from angry clients) until the moment that you complete it, and threaten yourself with showing someone that video. That'll get you moving.

6. **Keep your failure going until you're sick of it**. Did you decide to have salad for dinner tonight and end up with a frozen pizza? That's fine: force yourself to eat pizza for dinner the next six nights in a row, or until your dignity gets the better of you.

Chapter summary

- We live surrounded by temptation, and it would be silly to try to push it away. It's better to know where **your siren islands are** and prepare yourself for sailing by them.

- **Backup plans** are a good strategy for tackling potentially tempting situations.

- Some strategies I recommend to my patients for avoiding giving in to temptation include linking failures to **painful consequences** (such as losing money or experiencing shame), **surrounding themselves with the right people** or frequently reminding themselves **why they're doing what they're doing** instead of taking the easy way out.

Achieve excellence

I usually finish my books by congratulating readers on reaching the end and committing to their **true potential**. But before I congratulate you, I want to ask: have you already felt a **little change** in the way you view life? Have you realized that self-discipline is the path not just to getting yourself into gear but also to achieving fulfilment? If you have, then you've heard "the call". From the bottom of my heart, congratulations!

Now, don't let that energy dissipate, don't let anyone stand between what you've learned and **your drive to put it into practice**. Now is your moment. There is nothing more important in your life, believe me.

It's true that you still have work to do, but don't let that daunt you: start by assessing where you are now (I'm sure it's not as bad as you think!) and take a look at your life purposes. Those are **steps 1 and 2** of this book, and you can do them in less than a week. From now on, work hard, be consistent, improve your relationship with time and don't lose sight of the fact **your future is golden**.

Remember that at the beginning I told you that if you completed these seven steps and your life didn't improve, I would give you your money back? Well, I meant it. I'm that confident – not because my book is infallible, but because I believe in **the power of self-discipline to change everything**.

I should also warn you that my method has revolutionized the lives as many of my patients as well as my own, but the secret is not much more than **hard work** and **perseverance**. There's no magic potion to self-discipline in twenty-four hours – at least, as far as I know.

The good news is that you know you're perfectly capable of doing it, that a future you can be proud of awaits you – and that it's not too far away. In fact, your future starts **right now**.

In the words of Mark Twain: "the secret of getting ahead is getting started."

And in my own words: "Discipline yourself and you'll be happy!"

May strength and discipline be with you!

Daniel

Your opinion is very important

As I'm an independent author, your opinion is so important to me and to future readers like you. I would be hugely grateful if you would leave me **a review on your favorite store** to tell me what you thought of my book **so that I can keep on improving it**:

- What did you like best?
- Is there anything you felt was missing
- Who would you recommend it to?
- ...

www.danieljmartin.es/review/pod

A gift just for you!

Would you like to **read my next book completely FREE?** Scan the code below and **join my readers' club!**

Great surprises await: be the first to read my new releases, listen to my audiobooks for free, get signed and dedicated copies... and much more!

www.danieljmartin.es/readersclub/

Other books by Daniel J. Martin

http://www.danieljmartin.es/wide/books

www.ingramcontent.com/pod-product-compliance
Lightning Source LLC
Chambersburg PA
CBHW020719160726
47993CB00006B/2264